P9-CML-086

Blue Whale

The World's Biggest Mammal

by Molly Smith

Consultant: Jenny Montague
Assistant Curator of Marine Mammals
New England Aquarium
Boston, MA

New York, New York

Credits

Cover, ©Mike Johnson/earthwindow.com; 2–3, ©Francois Gohier/Ardeas; 4, Kathrin Ayer; 4–5, Seapics.com; 6, ©Tom Bean/Corbis; 7, ©Tom Bean/Corbis; 8, Kathrin Ayer; 9, ©Mark Conlin/Norbert Wu, www.norbertwu.com, (inset), ©Flip Nicklen/Minden Pictures; 10, ©Flip Nicklen/Minden Pictures; 11, ©Flip Nicklen/Minden Pictures; 12, ©Phillip Colla/Seapics.com; 13, ©Mike Johnson/Marine Natural History Photography; 14–15, ©Phillip Colla/Bruce Coleman; 16–17, ©Flip Nicklen/Minden Pictures; 18, ©Peter Howorth/Norbert Wu, www.norbertwu.com; 19, ©Mike Johnson/Seapics.com; 20–21, ©Mark Jones/Minden Pictures; 22L, ©Brandon Cole/Corbis; 22C, ©Yva Momatiuk and John Eastcott/Minden Pictures; 22R, ©Brian Skerry/Getty Images; 23BL, ©Flip Nicklin/Minden Pictures; 23TR, ©Patricio Robles Gil/Minden Pictures; 23BR, ©Flip Nicklen/Minden Pictures; 23BKG, ©Mike Johnson/Seapics.com.

Publisher: Kenn Goin
Editorial Director: Adam Siegel
Editorial Development: Nancy Hall, Inc.
Creative Director: Spencer Brinker
Photo Researcher: Carousel Research, Inc.: Mary Teresa Giancoli
Design: Otto Carbajal

Library of Congress Cataloging-in-Publication Data

Smith, Molly, 1974-

Blue whale : the world's biggest mammal / by Molly Smith.
    p. cm.—(SuperSized!)
Includes bibliographical references (p.   ) and index.
ISBN-13: 978-1-59716-385-9 (library bdg.)
ISBN-10: 1-59716-385-6 (library bdg.)
1. Blue whale—Juvenile literature. I. Title.

QL737.C424S65 2007

599.5'248—dc22

                              2006028813

For more information, write to Bearport Publishing Company, Inc., 101 Fifth Avenue, Suite 6R, New York, New York 10003. Printed in the United States of America.

10 9 8 7 6 5 4 3 2 1

Contents

Big Blue 4

Homes Around the World 6

Tiny Treats, Big Eats 8

There She Blows! 10

Two Tons of Fun 12

Way to Grow 14

The Buddy System 16

Loud and Clear 18

Gentle Giants 20

More Big Mammals 22
Glossary 23
Index 24
Read More 24
Learn More Online 24

Big Blue

The blue whale is the biggest animal that has ever lived on Earth.

Even the largest dinosaur was not as big!

A blue whale is about as long as a Boeing 737 airplane.

It can weigh as much as 25 elephants.

A blue whale can grow
up to 100 feet (30 m) long.
It can weigh up to 150 tons
(136 metric tons).

Homes Around the World

Blue whales live in oceans all over the world.

In the winter, the water gets very cold.

So blue whales swim to parts of the world where the ocean water is warmer.

In the summer, they swim back to the places they left.

Blue whales travel thousands of miles between their summer and winter homes.

Blue Whales in the Wild

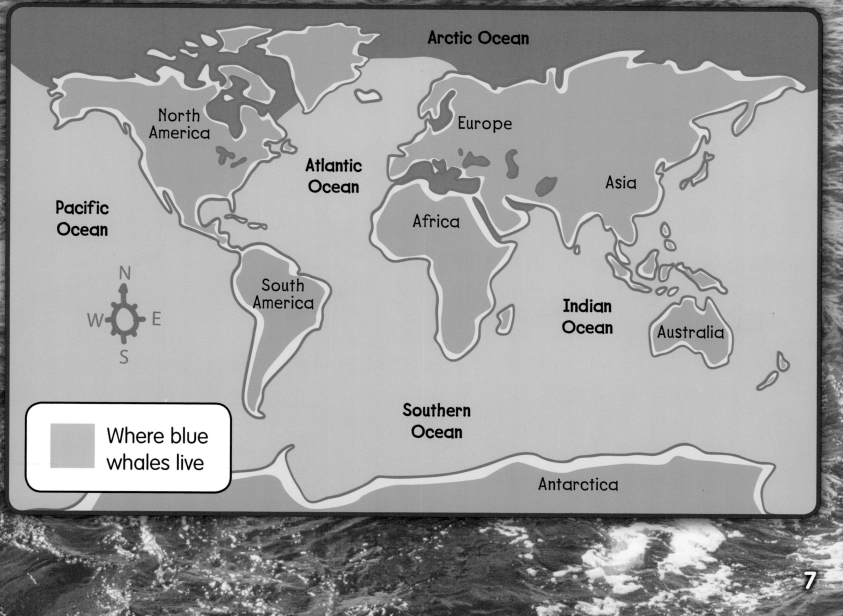

Arctic Ocean

North America

Europe

Atlantic Ocean

Asia

Pacific Ocean

Africa

N
W E
S

South America

Indian Ocean

Australia

Southern Ocean

Where blue whales live

Antarctica

Tiny Treats, Big Eats

A blue whale eats lots of tiny animals called **krill**.

The whale takes big gulps of water where krill are swimming.

Its tongue then pushes the water out through parts of its mouth called **baleen**.

Only the krill are left behind for the giant animal to eat.

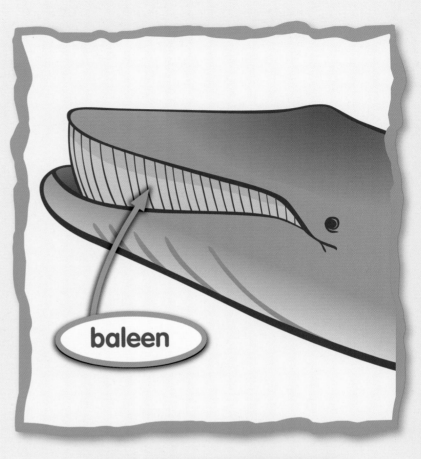

baleen

An adult blue whale can eat 40 million krill in one day!

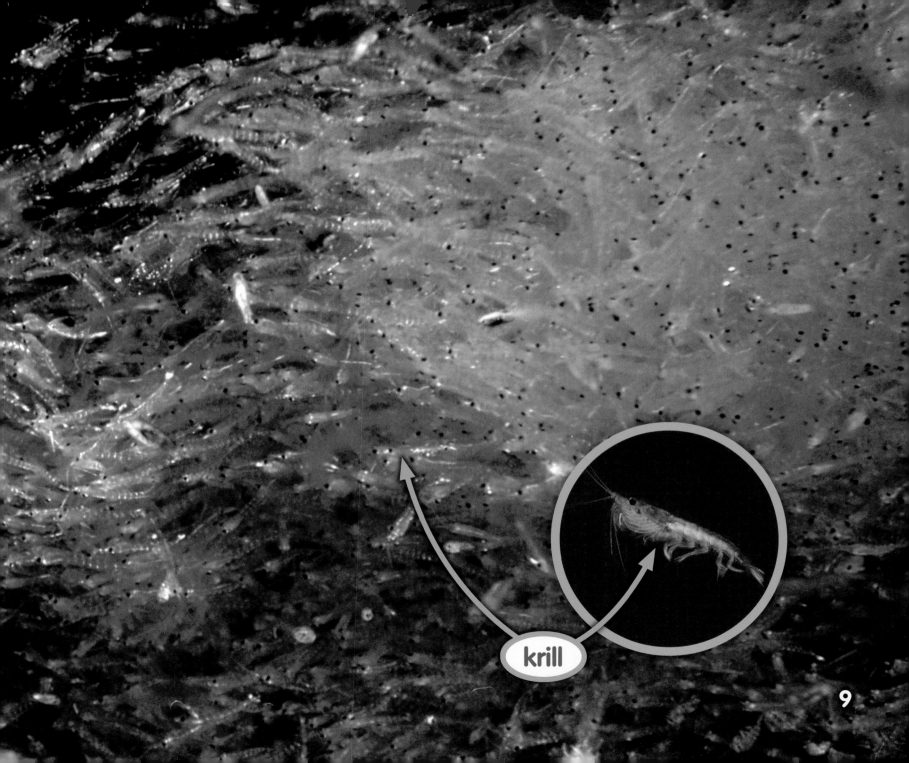

krill

There She Blows!

A blue whale breathes through two nostrils on top of its head called **blowholes**.

It takes a deep breath before it dives underwater.

When the whale comes back up, it shoots out old air from its blowholes.

A blue whale can shoot air up to 30 feet (9 m) high.

blowholes

Two Tons of Fun

A baby blue whale is bigger than an adult elephant.

It can be 25 feet (7.6 m) long and weigh 2 tons (1.8 metric tons) when it is born.

A newborn whale must quickly swim to the surface to get air.

Sometimes it needs a push from its mother.

A baby blue whale is called a **calf**.

13

Way to Grow

A blue whale calf stays near its mother for a year.

The calf drinks its mother's milk.

It can drink up to 100 gallons (378 l) a day!

It can gain about 200 pounds (91 kg) in one day, too!

Blue whales can live for about 80 years.

15

The Buddy System

Blue whales often travel alone or in pairs.

A pair may be a mother and her calf or two adults.

Sometimes whales will gather in large groups of up to 60.

Whales come together in places where they can find a lot of krill.

Loud and Clear

Blue whales can communicate with one another over hundreds of miles in the ocean.

They make deep, rumbling sounds under the water.

These calls are louder than the sound of a jet engine.

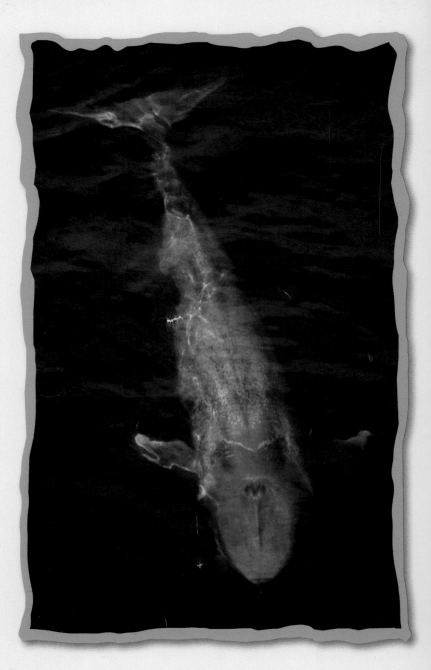

Blue whales are the loudest animals on Earth.

Gentle Giants

The blue whale is huge.

Yet it causes no threat to humans.

People once hunted blue whales until almost all of them were killed.

Today, laws protect the blue whale.

These gentle giants now swim freely in Earth's oceans.

There may be as few as 5,000 blue whales left in the world.

More Big Mammals

Blue whales live in the water, but they are not fish. Blue whales belong to a group of animals called mammals. Almost all mammals give birth to live young. The babies drink milk from their mothers. Mammals are also warm-blooded and have hair or fur on their skin.

Here are three more big mammals that live in the water.

Orca

The orca is the largest animal in the dolphin family. An orca can grow to about 28 feet (8.5 m) long and weigh 8 tons (7.2 metric tons).

Pacific Walrus

The Pacific walrus can grow to about 12 feet (3.6 m) long and weigh up to 1.8 tons (1.6 metric tons).

Manatee

The manatee can grow to about 10 feet (3 m) long and weigh up to 1 ton (.9 metric tons).

Blue Whale: 100 feet/30 m

Orca: 28 feet/8.5 m

Pacific Walrus: 12 feet/3.6 m

Manatee: 10 feet/3 m

Glossary

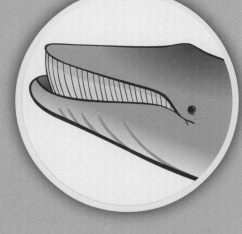

baleen
(buh-LEEN) parts of a whale's mouth used to strain small animals out of the water for food

calf (KAF)
a baby whale

blowholes
(BLOH-hohlz) openings at the top of a whale's head that allow the animal to breathe in new air and shoot out old air

krill (KRIL)
tiny shrimp-like animals that live in the ocean

Index

baleen 8

blowholes 10–11

breathing 10–11, 12

calf 12–13, 14–15, 16

food 8–9, 14

homes 6–7

krill 8–9, 16

life span 14

manatee 22

mother whales 12–13, 14–15, 16

orca 22

Pacific walrus 22

size 4–5, 12, 14, 22

sounds 18–19

weight 4–5, 12, 14, 22

Read More

Davies, Nicola. *Big Blue Whale (Read and Wonder).* Cambridge, MA: Candlewick Press (2001).

Malloy, Christine Corning. *The Blue Whale (Flip Out and Learn).* San Francisco, CA: Chronicle Books (2003).

Learn More Online

To learn more about blue whales, visit **www.bearportpublishing.com/SuperSized**